hindi KAY BOL

Yayyyy! It's Monday!
फिर आया सोमवार

यह किताब.......................की है।

This book belongs to ....

लेखन - प्रिया गुप्ता
चित्रांकन - मेघांश

This book is for my children, for they find joy in simple things. Also, I would like to thank every trash worker in the world.

यह किताब मेरे बच्चों के लिए है, क्योंकि वे साधारण में भी खुशी ढूँढ लेते हैं। हर कूड़ा कर्मी को मेरा धन्यवाद!

••• Priya...

Designed by 'www.arcreativewings.com'

www.hindikaybol.com
Follow us on FB / IG @ hindikaybol

ISBN Hindi Edition: 978-93-5426-433-7

ISBN Hindi-English Paperback: 978-93-5895-932-1

ISBN Hindi-English Hardcover: 978-93-5891-589-1

It's a Monday! There's something special today.

आज सोमवार है। आज कुछ ख़ास है!

We wake up at 7 o'clock every day. Today, my brother and I got up at 6 o'clock. Do you want to know why?

रोज़ हम सात बजे उठते हैं।
आज मैं और मेरा भाई छः बजे उठ गए।
पूछिए क्यों?

आज स्कूल भी नहीं जाना।
बाहर बरफ़ गिर रही है ना!!

There's no school today. It's snowing at last.

What made us get up so early?
Mom is quite amused.

फिर हम क्यों जल्दी उठे?
माँ भी हैरान है।

वे

We looked at the clock once more.

And then we heard it coming- "Vrooooooom!" Off we ran!

हमने एक और बार घड़ी की तरफ़ देखा।

आगे सड़क से आवाज़ आई - वरोउम्म्म! हम भागे।

We opened the window and sat wide-eyed.

We could see it far away.

Big, yellow, and strong – the trash pick-up truck.

हमने खिड़की खोली और ताक लगाकर बैठ गए।
वह दूर से आता दिख रहा था। बड़ा, पीला, और
ताकतवर-हमारा कूड़े का ट्रक!

It stopped right outside our house.

Its big arm came forward and emptied the trash can in its belly.

वह घर के बाहर रूका, उसका हाथ आगे आया,

और उसने हमारे कूड़ेदान को अपने अन्दर पलट लिया।

We were thrilled. The truck driver waved at us.

हम बहुत खुश हुए। फिर ट्रक ड्राइवर ने हमें बाय किया।

मेरा भाई सोचता है कि
ट्रक सारा कूड़ा खा लेता है!!
लेकिन मुझे पता है कि
वह कूड़ा कहाँ जाता है।

My brother thinks that the truck gobbles up the trash. But I know better where the trash ends up.

Landfill, where the trash decomposes under the earth.

हरे कूड़ेदान का कूड़ा लैन्ड्फिल में जाता है,
यानि धरती में दबाया जाता है।
नीले कूड़ेदान का कूड़ा रीसाइकल,
यानि फिर से उपयोग किया जाता है।

Recycling plant, where the contents are processed into new things.

कूड़ा कम से कम करें। धरती को साफ रखें!
जैसे हम अपने घर को रखते हैं।

Create lesser waste. Keep the earth clean.
Just like we keep our home!

Sort t

प्लास्टिक कप
Plastic cup

खाली गत्ता
Packaging box

मोटी प्लास्टिक
Thick plastic bottles

अख़बार
Newspaper

कूड़

ash!

टें!

काँच की बोतल
Glass bottle

दूध की खाली बोतल
Empty milk can

मैटल कैन
Soda can

केले का छिलका
Banana peel

Key to difficult words

सोमवार	Monday
ख़ास	Special
रोज़	Everyday
उठ	Get up / Wake up
पूछिए	Ask
बरफ़	Snow
जल्दी	Early / Quick
हैरान	Surprised
घड़ी	Clock
सड़क	Road

आवाज़	Sound
खिड़की	Window
ताक	Gaze
ताकतवर	Strong
कूड़े का ट्रक	Trash truck
कूड़ेदान	Trash can
कि	That
उपयोग	Use
साफ़	Clean
धरती	Earth

Hindi special letters

Some half letters combine with the next consonant and change shape.

Half ट+र = ट्र (tr) as in ट्रक

Half ड+र = ड्र (dr) as in ड्राइवर

Other half letters with र

Half प+र = प्र (pr)

Half क+र = क्र (kr)

Half द+र = द्र (dr)

Half ग+र = ग्र (gr)

Vowels / स्वर (swar)

अ	आ	इ	ई	उ	ऊ	ऋ
a	aa	i	ee	u	oo	ri
ए	ऐ	ओ	औ	अं	अः	
a	ae	o	au	am	ah	

Consonant / व्यंजन (vyanjan)

क	ख	ग	घ	ङ
ka	kha	ga	gh	ng
च	छ	ज	झ	ञ
ca	cha	ja	jha	ña
ट	ठ	ड	ढ	ण
ṭa	ṭha	ḍa	ḍha	ṇa
त	थ	द	ध	न
ta	tha	da	dha	na
प	फ	ब	भ	म
pa	pha	ba	bha	ma

य	र	ल	व
ya	ra	la	va
श	ष	स	ह
śa	ṣa	sa	ha

क्ष	त्र	ज्ञ
ksh	tra	gya

Priya Gupta is a published author of several children's books. She likes to create spaces for kids to embrace multicultural upbringing. Priya founded Hindikaybol with a vision to create high-quality bilingual Hindi-English books that represent South Asian culture and universal values. She lives in Connecticut, USA with her husband and two kids, her constant inspiration.

Meghansh is a painter and sculptor working in the field of art for the last 24 years. With strong narratives and visually powerful artworks, Meghansh expresses personal experiences of day-to-day life and his perception of Spirituality and connection with the Omnipresent, the Formless. He lives in New Delhi, India where he runs an art school, apart from participating in artist camps and art exhibitions.

Printed at Repro India Ltd.